D1612607

THE FIRESIDE BOOK

A picture and a poem
for every mood
chosen by
David Hope

Printed and Published by
D. C. THOMSON & CO., LTD.
185 Fleet Street, London EC4A 2HS.

SPEAK ON THESE THINGS

IF there be faith and love and charity,
   The shining wonder of a bluebird's wings,
If there is joy and beauty in your life,
   Speak on these things.

If there be trust when all men seem to doubt,
   A lullaby that some young mother sings,
A neighbour on whose goodness you rely,
   Speak on these things.

If there be majesty and truth and grace,
   A happy message that the postman brings,
The welcome visitor who comes to call,
   Speak on these things.

If there are golden rod-like tapers lit,
   An old grey wall where coloured ivy clings,
A garden where tall lilies scent the air,
   Speak on these things.

If there be beauty in a world of ill,
   A quiet valley where a church bell rings;
Where there is faith and love and little homes,
   Speak on these things.

Edna Jaques .

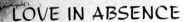

LOVE IN ABSENCE

TODAY you walk a London street
  While noisy traffic surges by,
With stony pavements for your feet,
  And houses crowding out the sky.

Your weary brain is filled with schemes
  That with your hurried steps keep pace,
Committees leave no time for dreams,
  The London look is on your face.

The roads I walk are country-sweet,
  And robins sing as I pass by,
Gold beech leaves rustle round my feet,
  Mountains are blue against blue sky.

Yet Love has so entwined us two
  These many years increasingly,
My thoughts are there in town with you,
  And yours are walking here with me.

You catch the belling of the deer,
  You see the road mount white and hilly,
And in this moorland peace *I* hear
  The rush and roar of Piccadilly.

Mabel V. Irvine

THE BONFIRE

THOUGH you've travelled the world
Both wide and far;
Though you cannot remember
How old you are;

Though you rode with the rest
In the Jameson Raid
(Or was it the Charge
Of the Light Brigade?);

Though you suffer from gout
And your joints are set,
There's a bit of the boy
Left in you yet:

So, as soon as the bonfire
Is fairly lit,
You trot down the garden
To do your bit . . .

And the gardener's grandson
Is heard to complain
That, what with the Colonel
And what with the rain,
He must light that old bonfire
All over again.

Reginald Arkell

SONG OF THE SEAWIND

HOW it sings, sings, sings,
    Blowing sharply from the sea-line,
With an edge of salt that stings;
  How it laughs aloud, and passes,
  As it cuts the close cliff-grasses;
    How it sings again, and whistles
    As it shakes the stout sea-thistles—
    How it sings!

How it shrieks, shrieks, shrieks,
  In the crannies of the headland,
In the gashes of the creeks;
  How it shrieks once more, and catches
  Up the yellow foam in patches:
    How it whirls it out and over
    To the corn-field and the clover—
    How it shrieks!

How it roars, roars, roars,
  In the iron under-caverns,
In the hollows of the shores;
  How it roars anew, and thunders,
  As the strong hull splits and sunders:
    And the spent ship, tempest driven,
    On the reef lies rent and riven—
      How it roars!

How it wails, wails, wails,
  In the tangle of the wreckage,
In the flapping of the sails;
  How it sobs away, subsiding,
  Like a tired child after chiding;
    And across the ground-swell rolling,
    You can hear the bell-buoy tolling—
      How it wails!

Austin Dobson

TEA

WHAT soothes our quivering nerves like balm
    When stabbed awake by the loud alarm?
What dulls the agony as we blench
At the ghastly thought of the getting-up wrench?

Beautiful tea
For you and me,
Sups of it,
Cups of it,
Beautiful tea.

What makes the visitor stay and chat
For another ten minutes upon the mat,
Politely pretending she does not see
Preparations in progress for afternoon tea?

Beautiful tea
For her and me,
Lots of it,
Pots of it,
Beautiful tea.

What bridges the chasms and fills the gaps
When anecdotes dwindle and platitudes lapse,
And the hostess discovers that every one knows
Quite three of her party are rivals and foes?

Beautiful tea
For each of the three,
Balming them,
Calming them,
Beautiful tea.

Delectable liquid—so dear to its drinker,
Inspiring the artist—a thought to the thinker,
Beneficient beverage—sipped as you see
By monarchs, celebrities, persons, and me.

Beautiful tea
For others and we,
Think of it,
Drink of it,
BEAUTIFUL tea.

Molly Capes

NOCTURNE

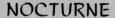

A SENSE of stolen joy is mine
  To leave the village sleeping,
And with the music of my feet
To wake the echoes down the street,
  Where ne'er a light is peeping.

'Tis fine to hear the steeple clocks
  With weary voice and hollow
Discharge their conscientious twelves
As if they knew within themselves
  Of easier hours to follow.

Beneath the dim poetic moon
  The houses seem enchanted;
Their unromantic yesterday
Is charmed a thousand years away,
  And each is beauty-haunted.

And even the thoughts that come to me
  The strangest shapes are taking,
And smack of dream and shadow too,
As if the night would claim her due
  From slumber or from waking!

Walter Wingate

SILENT WORSHIP

DID you not hear my lady
  Go down the garden singing?
Blackbird and thrush were silent
  To hear the alleys ringing.
O saw you not my lady
  Out in the garden there?
Shaming the rose and lily
  For she is twice as fair.

Though I am nothing to her,
  Though she must rarely look at me,
And though I could never woo her,
  I love her till I die.

Surely you heard my lady
  Go down the garden singing,
Silencing all the song-birds
  And setting the alleys ringing.
But surely you see my lady
  Out in the garden there
Riv'ling the glittering sunshine
  With a glory of golden hair.

Arthur Somervell

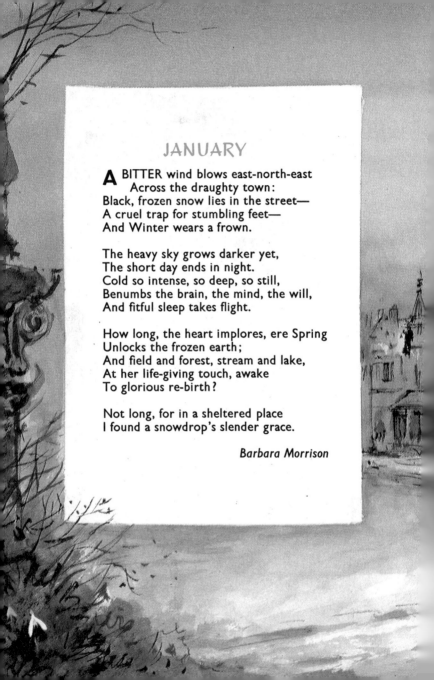

JANUARY

A BITTER wind blows east-north-east
    Across the draughty town:
Black, frozen snow lies in the street—
A cruel trap for stumbling feet—
And Winter wears a frown.

The heavy sky grows darker yet,
The short day ends in night.
Cold so intense, so deep, so still,
Benumbs the brain, the mind, the will,
And fitful sleep takes flight.

How long, the heart implores, ere Spring
Unlocks the frozen earth;
And field and forest, stream and lake,
At her life-giving touch, awake
To glorious re-birth?

Not long, for in a sheltered place
I found a snowdrop's slender grace.

Barbara Morrison

OAK BEAMS

ABOUT three hundred years ago—
The date I don't precisely know—
A builder lived who, for a joke,
Cut down a mighty forest oak,
And with the beams from off that tree,
He made a little house for me.
And so I see, in my oak beams,
Fulfilment of that good man's dreams.
In summer fair or winter bleak
Of beauty and of strength they speak.
Some houses that they make today
Are planned in quite a different way;
In ev'ry line they show the guilt
Of being badly jerry-built;
They will not weather wind and sun
Three hundred years, as mine has done,
And when they fall, as fall they will,
My cottage will be standing still.

I do not know my builder's name,
But I am grateful, all the same,
And though he did it for a whim,
I raise my humble hat to him.

A. A. Thomson

FEBRUARY

THE fields are bedded down with snow,
   Like blankets tucked about their ears,
As if the world had gone to sleep,
   But now and then a bush appears
Wearing a crown of purple gems
With scarlet berries on white stems.

The windbreak running to the lake
   Has snowy trunks like silver birch,
Even the weeds have hoods of snow,
   Like quaint old women in a church;
The hens have frosted beards and look
Like old men in a picture book.

Along the highway, muffled wheels
   Go by without a breath of sound,
The fence posts stand like sentinels,
   Wearing tall helmets diamond-crowned;
The mail man in his battered truck
Has drifted snow and ice to buck.

And yet I know that spring is nigh
   Although the wind is cold and raw,
The sky is softer than it was,
   The fields have started in to thaw,
Putting aside their winter dress,
To don their springtime loveliness.

Edna Jaques

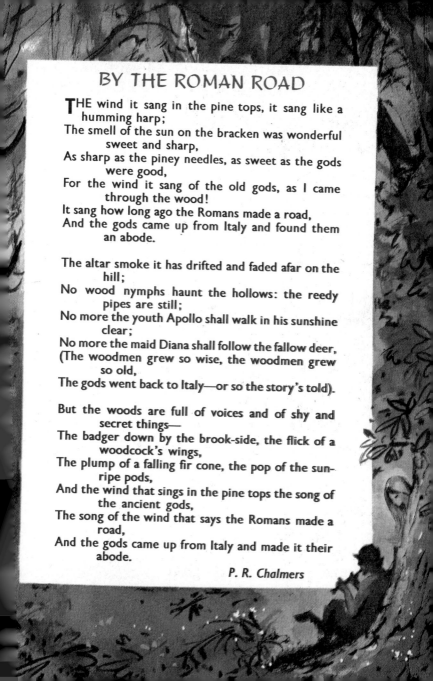

BY THE ROMAN ROAD

THE wind it sang in the pine tops, it sang like a
    humming harp;
The smell of the sun on the bracken was wonderful
      sweet and sharp,
As sharp as the piney needles, as sweet as the gods
      were good,
For the wind it sang of the old gods, as I came
      through the wood!
It sang how long ago the Romans made a road,
And the gods came up from Italy and found them
    an abode.

The altar smoke it has drifted and faded afar on the
    hill;
No wood nymphs haunt the hollows: the reedy
    pipes are still;
No more the youth Apollo shall walk in his sunshine
    clear;
No more the maid Diana shall follow the fallow deer,
(The woodmen grew so wise, the woodmen grew
    so old,
The gods went back to Italy—or so the story's told).

But the woods are full of voices and of shy and
    secret things—
The badger down by the brook-side, the flick of a
    woodcock's wings,
The plump of a falling fir cone, the pop of the sun-
    ripe pods,
And the wind that sings in the pine tops the song of
    the ancient gods,
The song of the wind that says the Romans made a
    road,
And the gods came up from Italy and made it their
    abode.

P. R. Chalmers

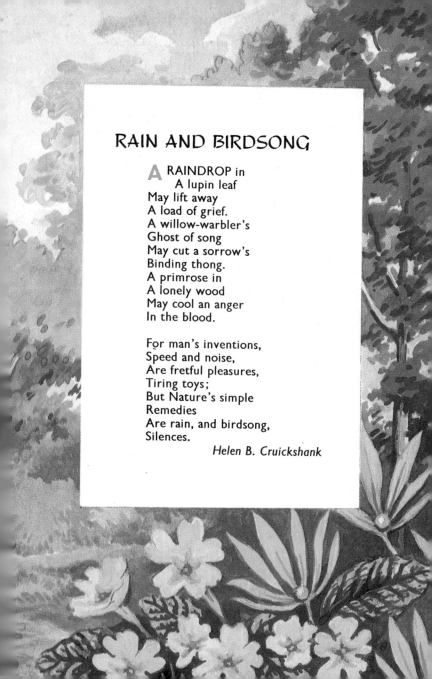

RAIN AND BIRDSONG

A RAINDROP in
A lupin leaf
May lift away
A load of grief.
A willow-warbler's
Ghost of song
May cut a sorrow's
Binding thong.
A primrose in
A lonely wood
May cool an anger
In the blood.

For man's inventions,
Speed and noise,
Are fretful pleasures,
Tiring toys;
But Nature's simple
Remedies
Are rain, and birdsong,
Silences.

Helen B. Cruickshank

THE NEW MOON

"NEW moon tonight!" you will hear them say,
    Turning their eyes to the glint of gold;
But this, as you know, is their quaint little way—
    For the moon she is centuries old!

She swings like a boat in the darkening sky,
    A boat that is gilded from stem to stern,
And "Turn your money!" the old wives cry—
    But every moon we have less to turn.

Yet saint and sinner and baron and boor,
    In log-built cabin or marble hall,
Happy-go-lucky and rich and poor—
    The brave little moon has a smile for all.

Alone in the drift of the leagueless heights
    Her course to the west she steers,
Rail-high with the lore of a million nights
    And the legends of all the years.

"New moon tonight!" So the people say;
    But the winds that cross her and croon,
They have sung in her silvery sails all day,
    And they know her, the old, old moon.

And the pine-trees listen and toss their heads
    And laugh in a splendid scorn,
For the old moon sailed by their cradle-beds
    Before the speakers were born.

Will H. Ogilvie

I LOVE YOU STILL

I LOVE you still! Nay, nothing less
   Has grown the passion that I told
In bygone times. I long to press
   You to my bosom as of old,
To kiss you once again, to see
   The tender look that used to fill
Your eyes, the smile that was to me
   A sheer delight. I love you still.

I love you still. E'en now, as then,
   The gowans curtsey as I pass;
The hawthorn's just as sweet as when
   We sat beneath it on the grass;
The twittering swallows dip and dart
   Along the burn, and by the mill;
And, just as then, my hung'ring heart
   Still clings to you. I love you still.

Andrew Dodds

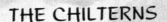

THE CHILTERNS

DID ever monarch lavish
    Such love upon a realm
As I confer on Chilterns
And all the fields of home?
I knew them in my childhood,
I loved them in my prime,
And always I shall haunt them
Until the end of time.
Thus when the world is older,
And I have passed away,
I'll tap a Chiltern shoulder,
And Chiltern man shall say:

"This hill this day is haunted,
I feel a spirit here,
Yet I am all undaunted,
Without a qualm of fear.
In truth, I feel the presence
Of some dead English man
Who loved these Hills as I do,
As only English can."
So shall I live immortal,
With never-failing breath
That draws from Chiltern breezes
The antidote to death.

J. H. B. Peel

THE SONG MY KETTLE SINGS

I HAVE a small blue kettle,
   A little homely thing,
And when I put it on for tea
   It always starts to sing.
It makes me think of little fields
   And hills all fresh and green,
Of tiny streams that slip along
   Their mossy banks between.

It has a note of wistfulness
   Like flutes all silver clear —
Perhaps it was the piping of
   Some fairy trumpeter.
It sings of quiet hidden pools,
   Of clouds and summer rain,
Of the grey waste of winter seas,
   Spring in the fields again.

Bird song and eventide . . . and still,
   Deep places of the earth,
All come to me and sing again
   Beside my glowing hearth.
I hear the piping of the lark,
   The sound of hurrying wings —
Here in my room . . . they whisper in
   The song my kettle sings.

Edna Jaques

ATHWART the sky a lowly sigh
    From west to east the sweet wind carried;
The sun stood still on Primrose Hill;
    His light in all the city tarried:
The clouds on viewless columns bloomed
Like smouldering lilies unconsumed.

" Oh sweetheart, see! how shadowy,
    Of some occult magician's rearing,
Or swung in space of heaven's grace
    Dissolving, dimly reappearing,
Afloat upon ethereal tides
St Paul's above the city rides!"

A rumour broke through the thin smoke
    Enwreathing abbey, tower, and palace,
The parks, the squares, the thoroughfares,
    The million-peopled lanes and alleys,
An ever-muttering prisoned storm,
The heart of London beating warm.

John Davidson

AN INVITATION

IF I should get to Paradise
   (And someone says she thinks I may),
I know what joys I would devise
   To pass the hours of endless day:

With fingers no more stiff as cranks
   That stumble as soon as they begin,
I'd play, with Michael, Cesar Franck's
   Sonata for the violin.

And you perhaps will join as well—
   When heavenly duties leave them free—
With Michael, Raphael, Gabriel,
   And play Schumann's quintet with me.

And if—supposing that in heaven
   Such things could be—we tire at last,
We'll hear " die Zauberflote," given
   By angels with an all-star cast.

These are the joys I hope will be
   Allowed us after our new birth:
Of course improved considerably,
   But very much like those of earth.

E. Keppel Bennett

CHRISTMAS TREE

YOU grew in the forest,
　　Dark and high
As you lifted your boughs
　　Towards the sky:
You were full of grace,
　　So proud and strong,
For you looked to Heaven
　　All day long.

Now you stand indoors,
　　To the children's joy,
And your boughs are laden
　　With lamp and toy;
There is love and laughter,
　　Joy so plain,
It's just like Heaven
　　All over again.

Margaret Bentley

I LOVE TO BE QUIET

I LOVE to be quiet so I can hear
   The sound of silence against my ear,
The beat of a heart in the quiet hours,
A bee's soft humming amid the flowers.

And if you remember, I know you've heard
The tender way that a mother bird
Talks to her fledglings as twilight nears,
And the first blue star of the night appears.

And sometimes deep in a quiet dell,
Where the leprechauns and the fairies dwell.
You can hear nearby in the purple glen
The marching song of the little men.

And a tree new laden with blossoms white
Rocks to itself in the quiet night,
And runs the scale of a special hymn
To a brand new nest in her highest limb.

For you'd never hear in the traffic's roar
The break of waves on a crystal shore,
As the tides come in like a sheeted ghost
To the rock-bound coves of a lonely coast.

So keep my heart to the quiet ways,
The soundless dark and the long still days,
Lest a heart would break if it couldn't hear,
The whirr of wings when the night is near.

Edna Jaques

THE LADIES OF ST. JAMES'S

THE ladies of St James's
  Go swinging to the play;
Their footmen run before them,
  With a " Stand by! Clear the way!"
But Phyllida, my Phyllida!
  She takes her buckled shoon,
When we go out a-courting
  Beneath the harvest moon.

The ladies of St James's!
  They're painted to the eyes,
Their white it stays for ever,
  Their red it never dies:
But Phyllida, my Phyllida!
  Her colour comes and goes;
It trembles to a lily,
  It wavers to a rose.

The ladies of St James's!
  They have their fits and freaks;
They smile on you—for seconds;
  They frown on you—for weeks:
But Phyllida, my Phyllida!
  Come either storm or shine,
From Shrove-tide unto Shrove-tide,
  Is always true—and mine.

Austin Dobson

WATCH THIS WOMAN

I KNOW a charming woman,
   And, every time she calls
She leaves my carpet on the floor,
My pictures on the walls.

She doesn't steal my silver,
Or ask me for a loan;
She doesn't use my fountain-pen—
She *always* brings her own.

But shew her in your garden
The treasures you have got,
And, if you turn your head away,
She'll pinch the blooming lot!

Reginald Arkell

THE YEAR'S FIRST LOVE

NOT a leaf upon the hedgerow,
 Not a primrose all the way,
The celandines must slumber yet
 For many and many a day.
Where the soft moist earth is breaking,
There the arums are awaking,
 And the Year's first Love stole shyly forth
 to greet me yesterday.

Ah, her hood was flecked with purple,
 Sweet she was, and passing fair;
And yet, as fits a humble maid,
 Her gown was sparse and bare.
She was meek as any lily,
Dainty as a daffodilly,
 And a store of Winter sunbeams she had
 garnered in her hair.

Oh, she came with magic meaning;
 Came with sun, and came with rain,
Herald of the radiant beauty
 That shall crown the woods again.
Little love, whose hair is golden,
What say they whose eyes are holden? —
 "Just a Yellow Coltsfoot growing by the
 gateway in the lane!"

Fay Inchfawn

WE MUST HAVE BEAUTY

WE must have beauty now and then,
  To feed the hungry souls of men.
Machines and gold is not enough,
  We must have more eternal stuff
To warm our hearts and satisfy,
  Before our souls and spirits die.

We must have roses in blue bowls,
  To feed the hunger of our souls,
The perfume of a daffodil,
  Some deep eternal want to fill;
Music to waft our spirits far
  Beyond the reach of any star.

We must have music's gentle flow,
  The tender light of candle-glow
In little rooms secure and bright,
  To hide us from the lonely night,
And arm ourselves by thought and prayer,
  Against frustration and despair.

For God has made us kin of Him,
  And so we see far off and dim,
The Promised Land we too may see
  Beyond the sky's immensity,
And so to bless and sanctify
  We must have beauty or we die.

Edna Jaques

THE HEART OF THINGS

AND could we live more near allied
　　To cloud and mountain, wind and tide,
Cast this unmeaning coil aside,
　　And go forth free,
The world our goal, Desire our guide,
　　We then might see

Those master moments grow less rare,
And oftener feel that nameless air
Come rumouring from we know not where;
　　And touch at whiles
Fantastic shores, the fringes fair
　　Of fairy isles;

And hail the mystic bird that brings
News from the inner courts of things,
The eternal courier-dove whose wings
    Are never furled;
And hear the bubbling of the springs
    That feed the world.

William Watson

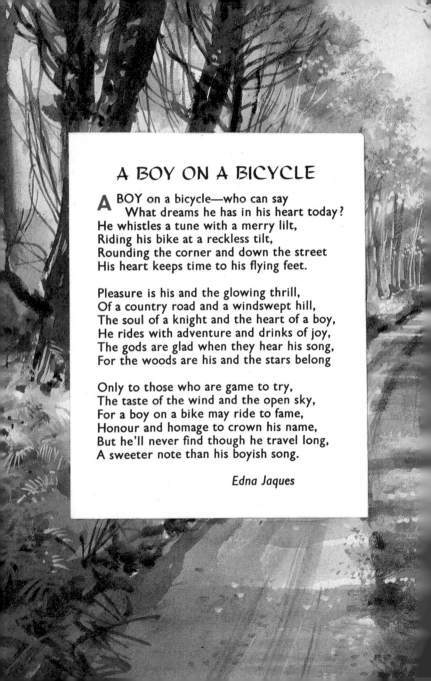

A BOY ON A BICYCLE

A BOY on a bicycle—who can say
    What dreams he has in his heart today?
He whistles a tune with a merry lilt,
Riding his bike at a reckless tilt,
Rounding the corner and down the street
His heart keeps time to his flying feet.

Pleasure is his and the glowing thrill,
Of a country road and a windswept hill,
The soul of a knight and the heart of a boy,
He rides with adventure and drinks of joy,
The gods are glad when they hear his song,
For the woods are his and the stars belong

Only to those who are game to try,
The taste of the wind and the open sky,
For a boy on a bike may ride to fame,
Honour and homage to crown his name,
But he'll never find though he travel long,
A sweeter note than his boyish song.

Edna Jaques

LITTLE SEA HOUSE

LITTLE sea house,
　When I found you,
The yellow poppies
　Were nodding round you.

Your blue slate hat
　That the four winds
Came to tug at
　Over the tamarinds:

I remember it well:
  The salmon nets drying —
Laugh, violin-shell,
  And cease crying!

For I will return
  Through the sea-haze:
I am sailing back there
  Always, always.

Hamish MacLaren

WAITING

ROOKS flying home,
    A sharp tang in the air,
Blue drifts of woodsmoke
In the garden there
Beyond the cottage windows;
Indoors, a log fire bright,
Table set for tea,
The lamp's warm light;
Soon the gate will click,
The children come.
Lovely in autumn
To be at home
In this quiet room,
Waiting joyfully
For all the noise and bustle
Of a family at tea.
Husband and children,
What could heart ask more?
Nothing more precious
In all life's treasure store!

Aileen E. Passmore

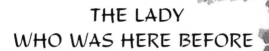

THE LADY
WHO WAS HERE BEFORE

THERE are some people that I hate;
  They gather round my garden gate,
Discussing, till I'm sick and sore,
The Lady Who Was Here Before.

They stand and whisper: " What a shame.
I'm thankful Mrs What's-her-name
Is dead, poor dear, and doesn't know.
She used to love her garden so."

" They've thrown away those lovely rocks
She got from Cheddar — and the box
She planted round her heart-shaped plots
Of heartsease and forget-me-nots."

" They've moved her salpiglossis bed,
And planted primulas instead.
They've put an ugly poplar tree
Where that nice privet used to be."

They'll get me so upset, some day,
That I shall spring at them, and say:
" This is *my* garden. GO AWAY!"

Reginald Arkell

THE LOTHIAN LAND

I HAVE a house in the Lothians—
  The middle of the three—
Its high windows look on the greenest fields,
  And God has given to me
A heart as glad as the fields are green,
  And that's how things should be.

On Turniedykes and Crichton,
  On Southside and Hagbrae,
I've watched the men out ploughing
  On many a winter day,
And see now what their ploughing's brought:
  This glad, green noon of May.

I've watched the crows in wintry dusks
   Go home to Currielea,
Winging low across the sodden fields,
   A pensive sight to me;
And now from my high window
   What a joy it is to see:

The cow park just across the road,
   The Moorfoots far away,
Between the undulant green fields,
   And woods as green as they . . .
There are no fields in the world as green
   As the Lothian fields today!

Andrew Dodds

WINDOW OF DREAMS

HE'S looking at the window — sure,
　　But what he sees are country streams
Half hidden in their tangled vines,
　　Tall trees through which the sunlight gleams,
A round pool like a pudding dish,
　　Where one can catch the glimpse of fish.

He hears the crunch of underbrush,
　　The sudden snapping of a twig,
The cushioned feel of moss and peat;
　　He knows the very place to dig
Where worms are juicy, fat and sleek,
　　Above the low bank of a creek.

He's looking at a glistening spoon
　　And sees in fancy a deep pool,
Like bottled ink . . . where speckled trout,
　　Lie in the shadows dark and cool;
A casting rod . . . a scarlet fly,
　　An arching dome of azure sky.

Trout baskets fill his longing heart
　　Almost to bursting as he feels
The taste of outdoors on his lips,
　　The jerky tug against his reels,
The thrill of landing one that fights,
　　The utter peace of country nights.

A window full of fishing gear,
Brought all this to him standing here.

　　Edna Jaques

LIGHTS

THE moon's glint on the water playing;
  A twin-beam on the roadway flung;
A bright arc on its standard swaying;
  The lanthorn by the alehouse hung.

A gleam over the green waves sweeping;
  The dancing lamps of a ship afar;
The brave glimmers their long watch keeping—
  The lower lights by the harbour bar.

But mine only, the warm red glowing,
  My own house on the hill set high,
And one waiting, this fond heart knowing,
  And ever the light of love in her eye.

Ian Chalmers

OLD BUTTON BAG

WHAT a gay host of memories
   That faded button bag contains,
Leading me back across the years,
   Down stony roads and quiet lanes,
Making me see as plain as day
The gentle folk of yesterday.

Here is a button of fine jet,
   My grandma had it on a basque,
I see her in her corded silk,
   Her face as rigid as a mask,
Waving her fan serene and sweet
In the old church on Maple Street.

This one was on my brother's coat,
   And I can see the little boy
That he once was . . . his chubby face,
   And eyes that sparkled from sheer joy,
Driving his dog on a red sleigh,
   Coming in rosy from his play.

So the old faded button bag,
   Is magic in a world of woe,
Giving me glimpses clear and bright
   Of that safe world of long ago,
When Love was there, serene and warm,
To shelter us from wind and storm.

Edna Jaques

WINTER RAINS

WHEN after weeks of winter rains
   The foggy air hangs still and wet,
When misted are the window-panes,
   And walls and sheets and cupboards sweat;
When chilblains itch in every shoe,
And the mind's furnished chambers too
Are damp and sodden through and through;

When meals are glum and shoulders ache,
   No match will strike or firewood blaze,
Fiddlestrings squeak and tempers break,
   No robin sings and no hen lays;
When paths are pools, and noses pearled,
And cats in kitchen fenders curled
Dream of a happier, drier world;

Then suddenly, when least we think,
   A bright wind breaks the mist, and there
The sun looks out above the brink
   Of piled-up clouds, stair over stair:
Glad then at heart are all live things,
Both small and great, on feet or wings,
Birds, boys and beggars, cats and kings.

R. C. Trevelyan

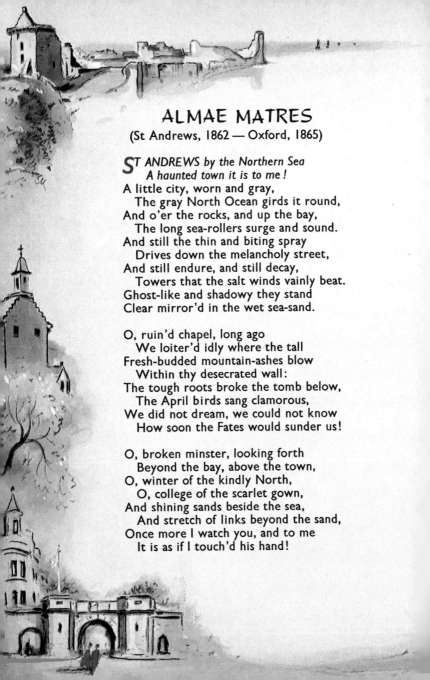

ALMAE MATRES
(St Andrews, 1862 — Oxford, 1865)

ST ANDREWS by the Northern Sea
　　A haunted town it is to me!
A little city, worn and gray,
　　The gray North Ocean girds it round,
And o'er the rocks, and up the bay,
　　The long sea-rollers surge and sound.
And still the thin and biting spray
　　Drives down the melancholy street,
And still endure, and still decay,
　　Towers that the salt winds vainly beat.
Ghost-like and shadowy they stand
Clear mirror'd in the wet sea-sand.

O, ruin'd chapel, long ago
　　We loiter'd idly where the tall
Fresh-budded mountain-ashes blow
　　Within thy desecrated wall:
The tough roots broke the tomb below,
　　The April birds sang clamorous,
We did not dream, we could not know
　　How soon the Fates would sunder us!

O, broken minster, looking forth
　　Beyond the bay, above the town,
O, winter of the kindly North,
　　O, college of the scarlet gown,
And shining sands beside the sea,
　　And stretch of links beyond the sand,
Once more I watch you, and to me
　　It is as if I touch'd his hand!

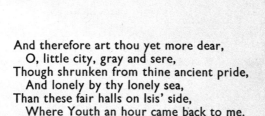

And therefore art thou yet more dear,
   O, little city, gray and sere,
Though shrunken from thine ancient pride,
   And lonely by thy lonely sea,
Than these fair halls on Isis' side,
   Where Youth an hour came back to me.

A land of waters green and clear,
   Of willows and of poplars tall,
And in the spring-time of the year,
   The white may breaking over all,
And Pleasure quick to come at call;
   And summer rides by marsh and wold,
And Autumn with her crimson pall
   About the towers of Magdalen roll'd:
And strange enchantments from the past,
   And memories of the friends of old,
And strong Tradition, binding fast
   The flying terms with bands of gold —
All these hath Oxford: all are dear,
   But dearer far the little town,
The drifting surf, the wintry year,
   The college of the scarlet gown:
St Andrews by the Northern Sea,
That is a haunted town to me!

              Andrew Lang

MARCH HARES

O, MAD March hares,
　The snows are past,
The winds are blowing,
　The clouds fly fast,
And you run mad
　'Mong the winter wheat,
With the clouds in your head
　And the winds in your feet.

O, mad March hares,
　I see what's wrong:
The field lies full
　Of tangled song,
And all your antics
　Among the wheat
Are just vain efforts
　To clear your feet.

O, mad March hares,
　The larks have you
In their snare of song,
　And they have me too:
Me by the heart,
　And you by the feet,
And the winds laugh low
　In the tender wheat.

Andrew Dodds

OPEN HEARTH

MY study has an open hearth,
    Flanked by a fireplace deep and wide;
With a secluded chimney-seat,
Where Ann and I can sit inside,
And as the winking firelight pales,
We tell each other fairy tales.

Here is a mighty iron jack,
Where once the family goose was basted;
Here is a salt box, where good wives
Made certain naught was ever wasted.
And here's a niche of shape so queer,
Where ancient Ephraims warmed their beer.

The oak-logs crackle, and the flames
Go blazing up the chimney-cavern,
Revealing pictures of old days
And tales that cheered a cosy tavern;
Glowing, as only firelight can,
On copper jug and warming-pan.

On summer nights no fire is laid,
But still we sit within the ingle,
And, gazing up the chimney wide,
We see the dusk and starlight mingle.
What more could heart of man desire
Than summer stars and winter fire?

A. A. Thomson

THE GREY MORNINGS

THE grey mornings I well remember,
   The grey mountains new waked from
  slumber,
The grey dews on the trees and hedges,
And in the grey distance the grey sea's edges.

Cool it was, sweet beyond telling,
The grey-green hay in the pastures smelling,
The grey meadows wet as a river,
The grey dew where the grass-blades quiver.

Grey gulls and the sea-grey swallow
Take the track that my heart would follow,
Home from the heat and the cruel weather,
That I and my heart might fare together!

Purple-grey are the wild hills showing,
Silver-grey is the west wind blowing.
O grey fields and grey hills behind you,
Would that my feet might follow and find you.

Katharine Tynan-Hinkson

PARTY DAY

WAITING, waiting, waiting
  For the party to begin;
Waiting, waiting, waiting
  For the laughter and din;
Waiting, waiting, waiting
  With hair just so
And clothes trim and tidy
  From top-knot to toe.
The floor is all shiny,
  The lights are ablaze;
There are sweetmeats in plenty
  And cakes beyond praise.
Oh the games and dancing,
  The tricks and the toys,
The music and the madness
  The colour and noise!
Waiting, waiting, waiting
  For the first knock on the door—
Was ever such waiting,
  Such waiting before?

James Reeves

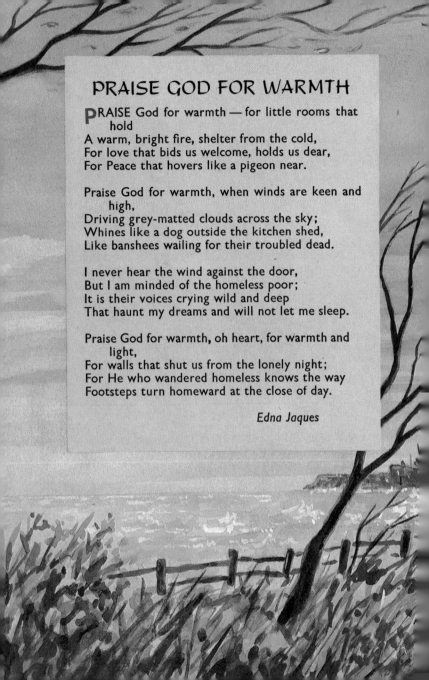

PRAISE GOD FOR WARMTH

PRAISE God for warmth — for little rooms that
    hold
A warm, bright fire, shelter from the cold,
For love that bids us welcome, holds us dear,
For Peace that hovers like a pigeon near.

Praise God for warmth, when winds are keen and
    high,
Driving grey-matted clouds across the sky;
Whines like a dog outside the kitchen shed,
Like banshees wailing for their troubled dead.

I never hear the wind against the door,
But I am minded of the homeless poor;
It is their voices crying wild and deep
That haunt my dreams and will not let me sleep.

Praise God for warmth, oh heart, for warmth and
    light,
For walls that shut us from the lonely night;
For He who wandered homeless knows the way
Footsteps turn homeward at the close of day.

Edna Jaques

THE HIGHLAND ROAD

FIFE was a shadow across the Firth
   When the Granton boat put out;
Over the sea and the solid earth
   The mist lay all about;
But a rousing wind from the Isle of May
   On the ruffled waters strode
And blew us a clear October day
   To ride on the Highland Road.

Tummel and Tay ran hand in hand,
  Farragon challenged us on
Through the old enchanted Atholl land,
  Grim heart of Caledon;
And the laughing Garry led us a dance
  By heather and rowans and rills
Till we saw the red deer watching askance
  On the grave Drumochter hills.

A minstrel wind from Badenoch sang
  Laments for the waning day,
As from the darkling Ericht the Truim sprang
  To carry us down to Spey,
By crags and corries and grey rock spurs
  Where the steadiest head may flinch,
Till evening fell on the Laggan firs
  And the sunlit birks of Insh.

Then thanks be given, whate'er betide,
  That still as heretofore
A man may waken in Morningside
  And couch him in Aviemore;
Thanks for the rare road running North
  And a day that gave its due,
From the mounting sun on the Firth of Forth
  To the moon on the Lairig Ghru.

Hilton Brown

SUNSET

FROM the calm firth the brightness slowly drains;
　　Steel-blue the water, darker blue the hills.
Above, one glowing, smoky band remains
That smoulders in a cloudless sky and fills
The tidal pools with crimson, soon to fade
Before the advancing shade.

Look and absorb, because the sun will set
Never again exactly as tonight.
I shall grow older, seeming to forget,
But, like that last, lone sea-bird's soundless flight,
Something has fluttered from my questing soul
Towards an unseen goal.

Douglas Fraser

THE WORD

MY friend, my bonny friend, when we are old,
  And hand in hand go tottering down the
    hill,
May we be rich in love's refined gold,
  May love's gold coin be current with us still.

May love be sweeter for the vanished days,
  And your most perfect beauty still as dear
As when your troubled singer stood at gaze
  In the dear March of a most sacred year.

May what we are be all we might have been,
  And that potential, perfect, O my friend,
And may there still be many sheafs to glean
  In our love's acre, comrade, till the end.

And may we find when ended is the page
Death but a tavern on our pilgrimage.

John Masefield

MIDNIGHT

THE air is dark and fragrant
  With memories of a shower,
And sanctified with stillness
  By this most holy hour.

The leaves forget to whisper
  Of soft and secret things,
And every bird is silent,
  With folded eyes and wings.

O blessed hour of midnight,
  Of sleep and of release,
Thou yieldest to the toiler
  The wages of thy peace.

And I, who have not laboured,
  Nor borne the heat of noon,
Receive thy tranquil quiet —
  An undeserved boon.

Yes, truly God is gracious,
  Who makes His sun to shine
Upon the good and evil,
  And idle lives like mine.

Upon the just and unjust
  He sends His rain to fall,
And gives this hour of blessing
  Freely alike to all.

                    R. F. Murray

THE JOKE

WHEN God had finished the stars and whirl of
    coloured suns
He turned His mind from big things to fashion
    little ones,
Beautiful tiny things (like daisies) He made, and
    then
He made the comical ones in case the minds of
    men
        Should stiffen and become
        Dull, humourless and glum:
And so forgetful of their Maker be
As to take even themselves — *quite seriously.*
Caterpillars and cats are lively and excellent puns:
All God's jokes are good — even the practical
    ones!
And as for the duck, I think God must have smiled
    a bit
Seeing those bright eyes blink on the day He
    fashioned it.
And He's probably laughing still at the sound that
    came out of its bill!

                    F. W. Harvey

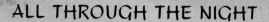

ALL THROUGH THE NIGHT

DEEP the silence round us spreading,
    All through the night;
Dark the path that we are treading
    All through the night.
  Still the coming day discerning,
  By the hope within us burning,
  To the dawn our footsteps turning,
    All through the night.

Star of faith, the dark adorning
    All through the night,
Leads us fearless toward the morning
    All through the night.
  Though our hearts be wrapt in sorrow
  From the hope of dawn we borrow
  Promise of a glad to-morrow,
    All through the night.

Anon.

AFTERNOON ON A HILL

I WILL be the gladdest thing
    Under the sun!
I will touch a hundred flowers
    And not pick one.

I will look at cliffs and clouds
  With quiet eyes,
Watch the wind bow down the grass
  And the grass rise.

And when lights begin to show
  Up from the town,
I will mark which must be mine,
  And then start down!

Edna St Vincent Millay

THE NEW GARDEN

IT is a most exciting thing,
   To take a garden in the spring:

To wonder what its borders hold;
What secrets lurk beneath the mould?

What kinds of roses you have got,
Whether the lilac blooms, or not;

Whether the peach tree, on the wall,
Has ever had a peach at all . . .

It is a most exciting thing,
To take a garden in the spring;

And live in such delicious doubt,
Until the final flower is out.

Reginald Arkell

MY SPECIAL DAY

I WATCHED as the postman drew nearer my
   door,
In anticipation of presents in store.
Somehow this moment seemed precious to me,
For birthdays *are* special when you're sixty-three.
So I took off my apron, then tidied my hair;
When I opened the door, he was already there.
"I've a parcel for Gittings," said he with a grin.
"I've knocked on their door, but there's nobody
   in.
Can I leave it here, please, until they get back?"
I nodded, then studied the bulge in his sack.
"I hoped there'd be something inside there for
   me.
You see, it's my birthday, and I'm sixty-three!"
But he seemed not to hear . . . The gate closed
   with a bang.
As I put down the parcel, the telephone rang.
My daughter was calling — a half-world away,
To tell me she loves me, on my special day.

Mary Brunsdon

THE SHEPHERD BOY'S SONG

HE that is down needs fear no fall,
 He that is low, no pride;
He that is humble ever shall
 Have God to be his guide.

I am content with what I have,
 Little be it or much:
And, Lord, contentment still I crave,
 Because thou savest such.

Fullness to such a burden is
 That go on pilgrimage:
Here little, and hereafter bliss,
 Is best from age to age.

John Bunyan

ACKNOWLEDGMENTS

To Heffer & Sons for "An Invitation" by E. Keppell Bennett; to Victor Gollancz for "Little Sea House"; to Mrs Veronica Gandy for "Love in Absence"; to Barrie & Jenkins for "The Bonfire", "Watch This Woman", "The New Garden", "The Lady Who Was Here Before", "Oak Beams" and "Open Hearth"; to J. Curwen & Sons for "Silent Worship"; to Leslie Brown for "The Highland Road"; to Donald Copeman Ltd. for "The Chilterns"; to Harrap & Co. for "Tea"; to Methuen & Co. for "By the Roman Road"; to Miss Wendy Ogilvie for "The New Moon"; to Allen & Unwin for "The Word"; to Sedgwick & Jackson for "The Joke"; to Lutterworth Press for "The Year's First Love"; to The Longman Group Ltd. for "Winter Rains"; to Wm. Heinemann Ltd. for "Party Day"; to Grant Richards for "The Grey Mornings".